PROTECTING THE ENVIRONMENT
OPPORTUNITIES TO VOLUNTEER

by Bernard Ryan, Jr.

D1411881

Ryan, Bernard, 1923-
    Community service for teens: opportunities to volunteer / Bernard
Ryan, Jr.
        p. cm.
    Includes bibliographical references and index.
    Contents: [1] Caring for animals -- [2] Expanding education and
literacy -- [3] Helping the ill, the poor & the elderly -- [4] Increasing
neighborhood service -- [5] Participating in government --
- -[6] Promoting the arts and sciences -- [7] Protecting the environment
- -[8] Serving with police, fire & EMS
        ISBN 0-89434-227-4 (v. 1). -- ISBN 0-89434-231-2 (v. 2). -- ISBN
0-89434-229-0 (v. 3). -- ISBN 0-89434-233-9 (v. 4). --
ISBN 0-89434-230-4 (v. 5). -- ISBN 0-89434-234-7 (v. 6). --
ISBN 0-89434-228-2 (v. 7). -- ISBN 0-89434-232-0 (v. 8)
        1. Voluntarism—United States—Juvenile literature. 2. Young
volunteers—United States—Juvenile literature. 3. Teenage
volunteers in social service—United States—Juvenile literature.
[1. Voluntarism.] I. Title.
HN90.V64R93   1998
361.3'7'08350973—dc21   97-34971
                                                                      CIP
                                                                       AC

Community Service for Teens: Protecting the Environment:
Opportunities to Volunteer

A New England Publishing Associates Book
Copyright ©1998 by Ferguson Publishing Company
ISBN 0-89434-228-2

Published and distributed by
Ferguson Publishing Company
200 West Madison, Suite 300
Chicago, Illinois 60606
800-306-9941
Web Site: http://www.fergpubco.com

Printed in the United States of America
V-3

CONTENTS

Introduction

Six out of ten American teenagers work as volunteers. A 1996 survey revealed that the total number of teen volunteers aged 12 to 17 is 13.3 million. They give 2.4 billion hours each year. Of that time, 1.8 billion hours are spent in "formal" commitments to non-profit organizations. Informal help, like "just helping neighbors," receives 600 million hours.

Each "formal" volunteer gives an average of three and a half hours a week. It would take nearly 1.1 million full-time employees to match these hours. And if the formal volunteers were paid minimum wage for their time, the cost would come to at least $7.7 billion—a tremendous saving to nonprofit organizations.

Teen volunteerism is growing. In the four years between the 1996 survey and a previous one, the number of volunteers grew by 7 percent and their hours increased by 17 percent.

Equal numbers of girls and boys give their time to volunteering.

How voluntary is volunteering? Only 16 out of 100 volunteers go to schools that insist on community service before graduation. Twenty-six out of 100 are in schools that offer courses requiring community service if you want credit for the course.

Six out of ten teen volunteers started volunteering before they were 14 years old. Seventy-eight percent of teens who volunteer have parents who volunteer.

Only 16 out of 100 volunteers go to schools that insist on community service before graduation.

WHY VOLUNTEER?

When teens are asked to volunteer, the 1996 survey revealed, nine out of ten do so. Who does the asking? Usually a friend, teacher,

(Courtesy: Paul Fusco/DEP Wildlife Division, State of CT)

Connecticut's Wildlife Division (Department of Environmental Protection) welcomed teen volunteers to work with members of the Association for Retarded Citizens of New Haven in a joint effort to build tern decoys. When the project was completed, the decoys were used at this tern-nesting beach in West Haven, Connecticut.

relative or church member. Teens gave a number of reasons for volunteering, regardless of whether their schools required community service. Their reasons included:

- You feel compassion for people in need.
- You feel you can do something for a cause that is important to you.

Exhibit 1

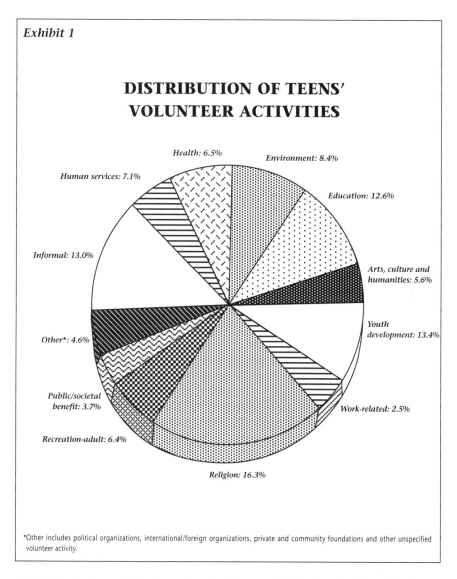

DISTRIBUTION OF TEENS' VOLUNTEER ACTIVITIES

Health: 6.5%

Environment: 8.4%

Human services: 7.1%

Education: 12.6%

Informal: 13.0%

Arts, culture and humanities: 5.6%

Other*: 4.6%

Youth development: 13.4%

Public/societal benefit: 3.7%

Work-related: 2.5%

Recreation-adult: 6.4%

Religion: 16.3%

*Other includes political organizations, international/foreign organizations, private and community foundations and other unspecified volunteer activity.

(Source: <u>Volunteering and Giving Among American Teenagers: 1996.</u> Independent Sector, Washington, DC, 1997.)

- You believe that if you help others, others will help you.
- Your volunteering is important to people you respect.
- You learn to relate to others who may be different from you.
- You develop leadership skills.

- You become more patient.
- You gain a better understanding of good citizenship.
- You get a chance to learn about various careers.
- You gain experience that can help in school and can lead to college admission and college scholarships as well as future careers.

VOLUNTEER FOR WHAT?

You can volunteer in a wide variety of activities. To get a picture of how teen volunteering is spread among various categories, see Exhibit 1.

WHO SAYS YOU HAVE TO "VOLUNTEER"?

Is "volunteering" for community service required in your school? It is if you live in the state of Maryland or in the city of Atlanta, Georgia. In fact, in many school districts across the United States you cannot receive your high school diploma unless you have spent a certain number of hours in community service. The number of hours varies.

Who makes the rule? In Maryland, the only state so far to require every high school student to perform community service, it is the Maryland State Department of Education. In most school districts, it is the board of education, which usually sets policies that meet the standards of the community.

If you have to do it, is it voluntary? And is it legal to make you do it? One family didn't think so. In 1994, the parents of Daniel Immediato, a 17-year-old senior at Rye Neck High School in Mamaroneck, New York, sued in federal court to keep Daniel's school from requiring him to spend 40 hours in community service before he could graduate.

(Continued on page 9)

(Continued from page 8)

Daniel's parents said the requirement interfered with their right to raise their child, that it violated Daniel's privacy rights, and that it was a violation of the Thirteenth Amendment to the U.S. Constitution. That amendment says:

> Neither slavery nor involuntary servitude, except as a punishment for a crime whereof the party shall have been duly convicted, shall exist within the United States, or any place subject to their jurisdiction.

The requirement for community service, said the Immediatos, imposed involuntary servitude on Daniel.

In its defense, the Rye Neck School Board argued that what it wanted was to get the students out into the community to see what goes on in the outside world. In the process, said the board, students would find out what it was like to have to dress appropriately for a job, be on time somewhere and have other people dependent on them. The emphasis was not on what the community would gain, it was on what the student would learn.

The court decided the school system was right. The Immediatos appealed. The U.S. Court of Appeals for the Second Circuit upheld the decision. The Immediatos asked the U.S. Supreme Court to hear the case. It turned down the request, as it does many appeals, without stating its reason for refusing.

Don't miss an opportunity that is disguised as a requirement.

—Karl Methven, Faculty Member and Head Coach,
addressing the Class of 1997, Proctor Academy,
Andover, New Hampshire, at the graduation ceremony,
May 31, 1997

"THIS ISN'T THE HALLS OF CENTRAL HIGH"

"If schools are going to demand that volunteering be part of success as a teenager," says Susan Trafford, president, Habitat for Humanity, Central Westmoreland, Pennsylvania, "I think the teens need to have, first, a selection in the volunteerism that they are going to do, and second, an understanding that this is a responsibility. This is the real world. This isn't the high school. This isn't the halls of Central High. I don't think we can just send them off and say, 'Now, here's your volunteer day.' They need a cause to go there, an understanding of someone, of what they will be contributing to. Sure, there are wonderful things that can be done. But don't send me six who have to do this before they can graduate."

CHAPTER ONE

What Is the Environment and Who Protects It?

*E*nvironment is everything that surrounds any living thing—any animal or plant. As a human being, you live in an environment that includes the air and its temperature, your food supply and the people and other animals in your life.

A plant's environment is also the air and its temperature, the soil or water it lives and grows in, and the animals that may eat it—including you. The same is true of every animal's environment.

Environmentalists describe two kinds of environment:

- *Abiotic environment.* Think of this as everything that is not alive. It includes the sunlight and temperature, water and soil and the chemical compositions of each, the weather and its humidity and wind, and the nonliving nutrients that nourish living things—such as protein and other elements that are essential to life.
- *Biotic environment.* This includes all living things—food, plants and animals, including you. More than that, it includes the associations and interactions among living things—the give-and-take of society among animals, and even the cultural aspects of life among humans.

What is *ecology*? It is the study of the relationships between living beings and their environments. An ecologist researches how environment affects the form, development and habits of animals or plants.

(EPA/U.S. Fish and Wildlife Division)

Some species face extinction from pollution or the destruction of their habitats. Once in danger of extinction, peregrine falcons have made a comeback in recent years thanks to conservation efforts.

You have to understand the environment around us in order to protect it and know how to protect it. If you don't understand it, you have a hard time doing that or justifying the need for protection.

—Director James Nolan,
Bent of the River Audubon Center,
Southbury, Connecticut

LIVING THINGS

Basically, the world of living things is divided into two types of living beings, or organisms: animals and plants. All are made of the same substance, called *protoplasm,* and almost all are composed of cells. A very simple organism may have only one cell, and it may be an animal or a plant.

Animals

Animals range in size from the tiniest bacterium you can see only under a microscope to the 150-ton, 95-foot-long blue whale. No one knows how many kinds of animals the world boasts, but the numbers include 800,000 kinds of insects, 30,000 types of fish, 9,000 bird species, 6,000 forms of reptile life, 3,000 different amphibians, more than 3,000 mammals ... and counting. They swim, crawl, walk and fly. Each has its own environment.

Plants

Life cannot exist without plants. The air you breathe gives you oxygen that was created by plants. The food you eat comes from plants or from animals that eat plants. You wear clothing made from plants—cotton or linen (from flax), or wool (from sheep that eat plants) or silk (from worms that eat plants). The house you live in, the chair you sit on, and the table you eat from were probably all made from a plant-product called *wood.* How many different kinds of plants are there? Like the total species of animals, no one is certain. Scientists estimate that there are more than 260,000 types of plants.

What do plants eat? Most create their own food by a process called *photosynthesis* from sunlight, air, water and the carbon dioxide that all animals exhale. So even as they feed us, we feed them.

Plant sizes range from the almost microscopic mosses growing on the California forest floor to the nearly 300-foot-tall sequoia trees that tower over them. Some living trees—the bristlecone pine, for example—are 4,000 to 5,000 years old.

▼

Each plant has its own individual environment.

Like the animals, each plant has its own individual environment. But scientists have classified six group environments or natural communities in which plants and animals live together. They are: tundras, forests, chaparrals, grasslands, savannas, and deserts.

Tundras. Mostly located above the Arctic Circle, tundras are the treeless land of North America, Europe, and Asia around the Arctic Ocean. Bitter cold except for a few weeks in summertime, their plants are low shrubs and wildflowers and the mosses beneath them.

Forests. One-third of our earth's land area is covered by forest growth—mostly trees, but also other plants. Forests can be classified into three main groups by climate: (1) in cold climates, coniferous forests, where evergreen trees dominate; (2) in the world's temperate zones, deciduous forests, where broadleaf trees shed their leaves each autumn; and (3) in the hot, humid lands near the equator, tropical rain forests, with trees that grow so lush that sunlight seldom penetrates to the ground, and lichens, orchids and vines climb high upon them.

Chaparrals. Where summers are hot and dry but winters are cool and wet, such as our American West, you find small trees and

(V. Harlow)

Some plants can survive only in a very specific environment. For example, these pond lily blossoms and leaves must remain above water, while their roots need to be in the mud, well below the water's surface.

shrubs in thick growths. Seasonal fires set by lightning help many chaparral plants to grow.

Grasslands. Across the Great Plains of the United States and Canada, farmers can grow rich crops of grains such as barley, oats, and wheat and graze their herds of livestock.

Savannas. These are like grasslands but include widely spaced trees and tall, stiff grasses. You can find savannas where winters are dry and summers are wet—in parts of Venezuela, Brazil, and Africa.

Deserts. In the heat and sands of deserts, you expect no plants—but there they are: cacti, creosote bushes, sagebrush, yuccas, Joshua trees and palm trees. Their environment forces them to live well apart, so they can extend long roots as they compete for whatever moisture is available.

In the heat and sands of deserts, you expect no plants—but there they are.

Certain plants have evolved to live in water. Their environments may be entirely underwater, or they may live with their leaves and blossoms in the air but their roots in the mud. You know them as water lilies and cattails, as eelgrass and duckweed. Like the three types of forest environments, the environments for each of the water plants consist of specific mixes of light, water, temperature and minerals from the soil or water.

SOME ENVIRONMENTAL CONCEPTS

When you volunteer to protect the environment, you are entering a specialized scientific discipline. The following are some of the words and phrases that naturalists use when they refer to common concepts about the environment.

Acclimatization

Most living things manage to adjust to changes in climate that come along to alter their environments. Many plants, for example, don't care if the temperature goes a little lower each night over a week or more, but may freeze and die if a severe drop occurs in one night. Naturalists call this acclimatization process *hardening.* The sheep's wool grows thicker when the climate turns cold and damp. Acclimatization is one aspect of adaptation.

16

(Courtesy: Paul Fusco/DEP Wildlife Division, State of CT)

Too many or too few species of animals can upset the balance of nature. Recently, the deer population in Connecticut has grown so rapidly that there is a food shortage among the animals. This overpopulation has also triggered the escalation of Lyme disease.

Adaptation

No two living creatures of the same species are exactly alike—with the exception of clones produced by human scientists. Animals and plants all show some variations, of size, color or personality. Those that are most likely to survive and reproduce are those that best adapt—based on their individual characteristics—to the environments in which they find themselves. If the environment changes and the living creature has poor adaptation, it dies out. Ask the dinosaur.

Balance of Nature

Think of plants and animals that live together in a given area as a community. If the numbers of animals and plants stay the same, the community is enjoying the balance of nature. But if you get too many, or not enough, of one plant or of one animal, you upset the balance.

A flood, a forest fire, a disease or pest, a bunch of people hunting or fishing, a housing development spread over acres of woodland and meadow—any of these can upset the balance of nature. Think of two classic upsets. One was the severe overhunting that reduced America's bison population from hundreds of thousands to only about 500 between the 1870s and the 1920s. Another is the urban sprawl that has invaded the environment of the deer since the 1950s while they were protected from hunters. The deer overpopulated while their natural food supply shrank. This upset the balance of nature. It also upset suburban homeowners, who found their expensive shrubs and rosebushes devoured. More recently, the growing deer population has fostered the spread of Lyme disease.

If you get too many, or not enough, of one plant or of one animal, you upset the balance.

Biodiversity

Biologists find great variety among organisms and environments. They see the protection of biodiversity—that is, sustaining the existing variety—as the most challenging aspect of protecting the overall environment. Think of two types of biodiversity:

1. *Species diversity* is the variety of species in a particular place or a particular group of organisms. For example, Costa Rica, a tiny tropical country, has some 830 bird species. That's more than you'll find in all of the mainland United States and Canada.

2. *Ecosystem diversity* is the variety of forests, lakes, deserts and other physical settings, with their respective plants and animals. What

is an ecosystem? It's a particular place with particular living things in it, and with particular nonliving things that the living things need. No two ecosystems are alike. If you destroy an ecosystem, you destroy the species that live only within it. Think of biodiversity as one key to the balance of nature.

If you destroy an ecosystem, you destroy the species that live only within it.

Habitat

An animal or plant's habitat is the place or environment in which it lives naturally. You can bet that the habitat of an octopus is not the same as that of an ostrich. But those of rabbits and raccoons in your backyard are not the same either. And a Vermont maple tree's habitat is nothing like that of a San Diego palm.

The habitats of animals and plants are artificially reproduced in zoos, botanical gardens and aquariums. With modern technology, we make the plants and animals feel right at home.

WHY DOES THE ENVIRONMENT NEED PROTECTING?

The answer to that question lies in two words: *pollution* and *us*. Human beings have polluted one natural environment after another. And since each of the elements of any environment—say, air, water and soil—is dependent on the others as well as on the animals and plants that live within it, pollution that hurts one part usually is bad for all the other parts.

The sections below describe the most common types of pollution:

Air pollution

One-fifth of the human population worldwide—and no one can say how many other animals and plants—is subject to dangerous levels of air pollution. Air pollution occurs both outdoors and indoors.

Outdoors. Cars, furnaces, dry-cleaning plants, and heavy industries—all send heavy smoke you can see and other vapors you cannot see into the air. The polluted air may contain tiny bits of matter, as well as natural dust, pollens and gases. One obvious type of air pollution is *smog* (a combination of "smoke" and "fog"), a hazy, brownish mix of gases and particles produced when the exhaust from motor vehicles reacts with sunlight.

The balance of nature in the atmosphere comprises nitrogen, oxygen, small amounts of carbon dioxide and other gases, plus some bits of solid or liquid matter. Air pollution interferes with the balance, producing several harmful effects. One is *acid rain,* the precipitation of harmful chemicals created when gases rising from the exhaust of cars, trucks and factories react with water vapor in the sky. Acid rain kills marine life and harms entire forests.

While ozone in smog is bad news, it helps us in the upper atmosphere by shielding the earth from 95 percent of the sun's ultraviolet radiation. But air pollution thins the ozone layer, letting in more radiation, which causes skin cancer and hurts plants.

As we send up carbon dioxide, methane and other gases, they let sunlight reach the earth but keep heat from escaping from the atmosphere. The result? Scientists suspect a *greenhouse effect,* raising temperatures worldwide and leading to melted glaciers, flooded coastal regions and severe droughts and tropical storms.

Indoors. Tobacco smoke, fumes from furnaces and stoves, cleaning chemicals, insulation and paint are considered pollutants. They can hang around and cause health problems unless the ventilation is excellent. Even the rocks under your house can produce *radon,* a radioactive gas that may cause lung cancer if inhaled in large amounts.

Water Pollution

In the balance of nature, water cleans itself through a natural process in which bacteria use the water's oxygen to digest wastes.

But groundwater supplying wells and springs from under the earth's surface, and surface water in lakes and streams, can be polluted by oils, metals, toxic chemicals and sewage. Polluted water not only hurts plants, birds and wild animals, but it also kills many people each year, most of them in developing countries.

Soil Pollution

The earth's healthy soil, which nourishes our food supply, counts on fungi, bacteria, and small animals to process wastes and provide nutrients that plants need. But human beings pollute the soil by applying too much fertilizer and pesticides, irrigating fields poorly, and contaminating the areas around mining and smelting operations.

Solid Waste

You see it everywhere. Junked cars, empty cans and bottles, a zillion plastic shapes, enough paper to stack to the moon—solid waste is a tough problem. Why? Most disposal methods hurt the environment. Open dumps welcome rats and spread disease; landfills let pollution seep into the groundwater; burning, even in incinerators, creates air pollution.

WHO PROTECTS THE ENVIRONMENT?

Two groups work to protect the environment: governments and private organizations. Governments pass laws and regulations and try to enforce them. Private organizations lobby to get laws passed. They also carry on scientific studies of the environment and maintain efforts to conserve it.

Government

The U.S. government's Environmental Protection Agency (EPA) sets standards and works with state and local governments to control

21

(Courtesy: S.C. Delaney/U.S. Environmental Protection Agency)

Government agencies and private organizations protect the environment by keeping beach areas clean with the help of teen volunteers, who pick up cans and bottles left there by picnickers.

pollution. State Departments of Environmental Protection (DEPs) also work under state regulations and cooperate with local conservation commissions from community to community.

The Clean Air Act of 1970 regulates how much air pollution may be released by motor vehicles and industry. The Clean Water Act of 1972 controls the release of harmful chemicals into rivers and other waterways.

Most communities now have laws requiring a builder or developer to perform an *environmental impact study* before any proposed new construction may begin. Particular care is taken to protect wetlands and the natural habitats of wildlife. Some cities and towns appoint or elect members of conservation commissions or wetlands commissions, or both, to review construction proposals and approve or deny them.

Local, state and national parks and refuges also protect the environment, often with regulations on where you may hike, camp or cook and how many of you may invade the place at any one time.

Recycling has become a household word, but no national recycling law has yet been passed. Most states, however, have passed some regulations, as have many local communities. The rules vary from town to town. How does recycling help protect the environment? It reduces the amount of waste—with its pollution of air, soil, and water—that we force onto the environment and reduces the need to manufacture new products.

Private Organizations

Protecting the environment is not a new idea, though many organizations have sprung up in the last 30 years. Among major national and regional groups are:

- American Forests. Founded in 1875, it works to advance the intelligent use and preservation of forests.

(Courtesy: Paul Fusco/DEP Wildlife Division, State of CT))

These Scouts volunteered to help Connecticut's Wildlife Division (Department of Environmental Protection) build a floating rest platform for waterfowl.

- American Oceans Campaign (AOC). Since 1987, this group has promoted the protection of the world's coastal waters.
- Friends of the Earth. Dedicated to protecting biodiversity and keeping our planet from environmental disaster, this organization was founded in 1969.

24

- Greenpeace U.S.A. This group, founded in 1971, monitors such environmental concerns as the greenhouse effect and waste-dumping research, lobbying and media campaigns.
- Hudson River Sloop *Clearwater*. Afloat since 1964, it promotes the restoration and preservation of the Hudson River and related waters.
- Keep America Beautiful. Since 1951, this program has fostered cooperation among government, business and the public to improve the handling of waste.
- Kids For A Clean Environment (Kids F.A.C.E.). This national group encourages children to organize and implement programs to protect the environment. It was founded in 1989.
- Land Trust Alliance (LTA). This umbrella association of local, regional and national land conservation organizations has worked since 1982 to increase the number of land trusts. It sets operating standards for land trusts across the United States.
- National Audubon Society. Since 1905 this well-known group has worked to conserve and restore natural ecosystems.
- National Wildlife Federation. An amalgamation of 45 state and territorial organizations, the group has been working since 1936 to conserve wildlife and other natural resources.
- The Nature Conservancy. Dedicated since 1951 to preserving the biodiversity of natural land and water areas, it is the nation's largest land trust (see below).
- Rainforest Action Network. An activist group founded in 1985, the network tackles such issues as logging and cattle ranching in rain-forest areas.
- River Network. Since 1988, it has supported local, state and regional advocates of rivers and watersheds.
- Sierra Club. Founded in 1892 by naturalist John Muir, the club

(Courtesy: Kids F.A.C.E., Nashville, TN)

Kids For A Clean Environment (Kids F.A.C.E.) was founded in 1989 by nine-year-old Melissa Poe and six other members, in Nashville, Tennessee. Currently, the group has more than 300,000 members throughout the United States. During the summer of 1995, two teens, Jennifer Morgan and Rachel Jones, plant cattails at a wetlands area in Salt Lake City, Utah.

has devoted itself to the study and protection of the earth's scenic and ecological resources.

- Student Conservation Association (SCA, Inc.). This group offers educational programs for high school and college students in national parks and forests. It was founded in 1957.
- Tree Musketeers. Since 1987, this national organization has supported young people in dealing with their hometown environmental problems.

Local Groups

In addition to government and private organizations, there are local groups such as land trusts and arboretums.

Land Trusts. These are privately sponsored and nongovernmental. They are legally incorporated nonprofit organizations that hold and manage land that they buy or that is donated to them. They are able to protect land—in effect, they protect ecosystems—from developers and others who want to change the land by constructing buildings or highways, or by mining or lumbering operations.

Arboretums. These are well-landscaped botanical gardens, but think of them also as outdoor laboratories. Usually they are filled with a variety of trees, shrubs and other plants, all carefully labeled and arranged by species. Experiments in developing rare plants or new varieties are carried on in many arboretums, and most are open to the public.

CHAPTER TWO

What You'll Do as a Volunteer

*T*he types of work you can do as an environmental volunteer range from helping to teach younger kids about the wonders of nature to lobbying to prevent developers, industrial corporations or government agencies—local, state and national—from destroying ecosystems. The work is of two basic types which may overlap:

1. *Actual involvement with the environment itself.* This type of work gives you a greater understanding of nature and an opportunity to help it to do its natural thing.

2. *Involvement with activist groups.* In this case you work to improve everyone's understanding of the environment and to influence the opinions of those who make decisions that affect the environment.

You can volunteer at any age. Elementary school boys and girls have started national programs to save the environment, then continued their interest and hard work all the way through high school. Some have even extended their efforts beyond graduation. When it comes to protecting the environment, any teenager can be powerful.

The range of things you can do is wide. Take it from Sage Rockermann, who "graduated" from being a high school volunteer to the director of the Sierra Student Coalition (SSC) in 1997 while she was in college. "Anyone can volunteer," she says. "Different skills and different qualifications will probably have an impact on what it is you are

Elementary school boys and girls have started national programs to save the environment.

(Courtesy: Tree Musketeers, El Segundo, CA)

At this Water Resources Festival, 13-year-old Marisa Smith of Tree Musketeers conducts "homeless baby tree" adoptions. Youngsters who promise to plant and care for a tree are given an adoption certificate.

volunteering for. Depending on what a student's interests and skills are, we can tailor their voluntary experience to what they enjoy," Sage explains. The SSC has an entire range of different types of opportunities for volunteers—from students who want to organize and run a campaign of student volunteers across the country to those who help out with such office work as answering the phone or filing.

Sage notes that students are interested in various issues. "There are people concerned about clean air or clean water. Some like to deal with urban environmental health issues and others like to work on wilderness," she points out.

Let's look at some of the things you can do, as a volunteer, to help protect the environment. In almost all cases, your work will be not only helpful in its own right but also quite valuable as an extension of the work of adults on the professional paid staffs of organizations.

Volunteer hours and other in-kind contributions of goods and services are as valuable to a nonprofit as dollars. [At Tree Musketeers] we can actually use the value of volunteerism and other in-kind gifts to "match" grants, and report them to the IRS as if donation checks had arrived. After all, if volunteers didn't perform a job, someone would have to be paid to do it.

—*TrunkLine,* **The Hometown Newsletter of Tree Musketeers, spring 1997**

OPPORTUNITIES IN YOUR COMMUNITY

There are many ways you can protect the environment—right in your community. For example, you can volunteer to help with recycling projects, litter collection or educating others through study outings.

Recycling

In your city or town, you can volunteer at a recycling center on those days, usually at least a couple of times a year, when people can bring in anything they want to get rid of—bundles of newspapers, magazines and other paper, hazardous waste materials such as paint, oil and strong cleaning agents, whatever. You help unload cars and show people where to take the stuff. In effect, you make people feel good about coming to the center. You help control their habit of tossing everything willy-nilly into garbage that is dumped in landfills where, sooner or later, it adds to the pollution of our environment.

Some communities are still just coming into the recycling age. Teens who understand the importance of protecting the environment are helpful in educating people about the recycling process. In West Haven, Connecticut, an environmental center has organized highschool students to go into housing complexes for the elderly and teach the seniors about how to reduce the amount of waste the environment is forced to accept. In El Segundo, California, teens were the leaders in implementing the curbside recycling program when it began in 1997, teaching people what must be sorted from what—plastics, glass (clear or colored), metals and paper (newsprint versus direct mail, etc.).

Teens who understand the importance of protecting the environment are helpful in educating people about the recycling process.

Litter Collection

Is roadside litter a challenge where you live? It is in most communities. It not only looks ugly, but it adds to water and soil pollution as well. If you join an environmental group, you can give a Saturday or Sunday once in a while to litter collection, picking up the cans, bottles, Big Mac boxes and other trash that thoughtless people toss out of car windows.

Study Outings

Inner-city kids don't get much chance to learn about the environment beyond city limits—unless they live where the Sierra Club runs Inner City Outings (ICO) or where some similar program is available. As a Sierra Club member, you can participate as a youth leader. Or you can organize a program of outings for the city where you live.

ICO takes elementary-school-age kids on trips to explore their nonurban environment. "We're hiking, canoeing, kayaking, looking at bugs and flowers and all that good stuff," says Beth Gardner, director of Sierra Club ICO in Seattle, Washington. "Kids who have been coming on the trips have stepped up to the plate to be youth leaders. They help organize the trips, run meetings, tell the kids where we're going, what we'll be doing, what kind of gear to bring. On the trip, they know how to set limits more successfully than we can with their peers."

We take third- and fourth-graders on a variety of outings like sledding, canoeing, hiking, camping—anything to get them outdoors and teach them about the environment. We even went on a rafting trip to watch bald eagles last winter.

**—High school senior Laura Mason,
Sierra Club Inner City Outings, Seattle, Washington**

Here are a few other examples of what you can do in your community:

- Students in Souderton High School in Pennsylvania built a demonstration home to show people how to make their own homes more environmentally friendly. The home is equipped with such examples of environmental technology

(Courtesy: Faye Ford/Marian High School, Omaha, NE)

Students from Marian High School in Omaha, Nebraska, set up a complete ecosystem to learn how important conservation is by practicing it on a local level. Here students prepare a thicket for mulching.

(Courtesy: Faye Ford/Marian High School, Omaha, NE)

Marian High School students place wood duck houses next to the wetlands as part of their ecosystem project.

as a composting toilet, insulation made from newspapers and carpet made from soda bottles.

- In Omaha, Nebraska, Marian High School juniors started digging in 1993. They set up a complete ecosystem—with native bushes, trees and prairie grass—that includes a woodlot, dam and pond. It is maintained by student volunteers.

- Students in the environmental club at Huntington Area Middle School in Pennsylvania designed and built a wetland on school property. The area provides the school with an outdoor laboratory that shows how urban wetlands can help control storm-water runoff and improve water quality.

LOBBYING EFFORTS

The Sierra Club is well known for its lobbying to protect the environment. Its SSC, which is entirely student run and has chapters in high schools and colleges across the country, leads efforts at local, regional and national levels. Sage Rockermann, the group's director, reports on a national campaign that began in the summer of 1997: "We launched an educational campaign about American public lands and the dangers that they face and what we can do about that. We will be sponsoring slide shows all over the United States. The shows will feature pictures of public lands from places like Utah and the West, Maine and New Hampshire, and will explain the dangers that these areas are facing. The shows will also provide contact information for those interested in learning more about what they can do to preserve public lands."

Lobbying takes planning and practice. If you are a member of the SSC, you find that out, for example, in working on a campaign to develop better relationships between environmentalists and family farmers. "Traditionally," says Alexis Goldstein, a Sierra Student Coalition member in Maryland, "the SSC has talked in the past with family farmers about using pesticides. So they were kind of on opposite sides. Now factory farms have come along. The factory farms aren't family farms. They're giant operations that take business away from the private families. Now a factory farm has tried to build a pig farm in Maryland. Factory farms, and especially pig farms, are environmental disasters. They produce all this waste, and it's a big mess. So the environmentalists started banding together with the local family farms to fight the factory farms. What we, the environmentalists, are doing is having a lot of practice sessions to find the best ways to develop better relationships with the family farmers."

We've fought against a giant incinerator being built very close to my house. And we've been trying to stop a huge road that's going to be plowing through everything—wetlands, forest—that's just five feet away from houses.
—High school senior Malka Fenyvesi,
Sierra Student Coalition,
Montgomery County, Maryland

Bear in mind that when you lobby, you don't always win. In 1997, Alexis Goldstein worked with the Montgomery County [Maryland] Student Environmental Activists (MCSEA) during her sophomore year in high school, trying to prevent a change in what was known as "the Dolphin Death Bill." The bill restricted the sale of tuna caught by Mexican fishermen using outdated methods in which dolphins were netted when tuna swam, as they like to do, beneath them. "Because of American restrictions," says Alexis, "they couldn't sell the tuna in the United States because they were caught using that method. They wanted us to change our regulations so they could trade with us. It was a big worldwide issue, mostly to do with Mexico. We fought it, but we didn't win. The change was passed in Congress."

HELPING STAFF AND ADMINISTRATION

In the office of an environmental organization, you can put typing, filing and data management skills to work. Craig Chancellor,

(Courtesy: Gail Church/Tree Musketeers, El Segundo, CA)

In most environmental organizations, office work can be just as important as field work. Tammy Smith has written numerous articles on the environment for various publications. Here she is finishing an article for the El Segundo Herald *at Tree Musketeers headquarters in El Segundo, California.*

for example, gave two days a week in the summer of 1997, when he was 14, as "a self-declared computer geek" at Tree Musketeers headquarters, managing the organization's data bank.

Such experience helps you learn the system in the particular organization where you are working. Let Gail Church, executive director of Tree Musketeers, explain why this is valuable. "In most cases," she says, "when an organization says it's empowering young people to do something, it means it's teaching them to plant a tree. But the kids will never really be empowered if they don't know how to do a timeline or a budget or have telephone manners. Those are the skills necesary to get to the point where you're ready to plant the tree."

Your office work may be like that of Kate Sands and Sara Colangelo. They worked together in the summer of 1997, before their senior year in high school, helping the Connecticut headquarters of The Nature Conservancy compile a history of all the research that had been done since the 1960s at all the nature preserves in the state.

Another key office job is helping with fund-raising.

Another key office job is helping with fund-raising. You may be asked to help assemble mailing lists and telephone lists. One of Kate's jobs at The Nature Conservancy was to organize and file newspaper clippings on major companies in Connecticut that the conservancy might solicit for donations.

SCIENTIFIC AND FIELD WORK

There are many opportunities to volunteer "in the field" to help protect the environment. The United States Bureau of Land Management uses many volunteers—over 20,000 each year—in several different ways. Volunteers help protect and restore streams, wildlife habitat, plant communities and ecosystems. Bureau of Land Management volunteers also serve as hiking leaders, youth group leaders, campground hosts and field guides. Some volunteers get the chance to write articles or take photographs for the Bureau's publications. Many also get an opportunity to work with animals at country fairs and horse shows.

Volunteer opportunities with Bureau of Land Management are open to high school and college students, as well as adults of any age. Teens under eighteen need to get written consent from a parent or guardian. Volunteers can work as many hours as they like or are needed. Most Bureau activities are concentrated in the West, primarily in the states of Alaska, Arizona, California, Colorado, Idaho, Montana, Nevada, New Mexico, Oregon, Utah, and Wyoming.

Earthwatch is another organization that offers volunteers field experience. Earthwatch is a worldwide nonprofit organization working to improve the planet in several ways. Since it was founded in 1972, it has had more than 50,000 volunteers work on its projects. Earthwatch volunteers can choose from a long list of programs in a wide range of fields, including animal behavior, archaeology, ecology, dinosaurs, endangered species, rain forests and wildlife management. In 1997, Earthwatch sponsored 140 projects in 51 countries and 21 states.

Earthwatch projects usually run from one to three weeks in locations around the world. Though the projects are open to high school and college students as well as adults, high school students need to be at least sixteen and have a high level of maturity. Keep in mind, too, that most Earthwatch field projects require volunteers to pay for their accommodations as well as the airfare to a project site. Costs for accommodations, which generally include room and board, range from $600 to $2,200; the volunteeer must arrange his or her own air travel.

Earthwatch also offers intern positions that combine both office and field experience. Though the internships are generally geared toward college students, some can be filled by mature high school students. Intern duties include fundraising, research, telephone work and some fieldwork. The intern positions are available at the Earthwatch headquarters in Boston and at its branch office in the Los Altos/San Francisco area. Though interns are not paid, for every hour worked they earn a $5 credit toward a project expedition.

TEENS BRING ENERGY TO ENVIRONMENTAL PROJECTS

"We had a 15-year-old boy not long ago helping with a butterfly atlas project that the Department of Environmental Protection was doing," says James Nolan, director of Bent of the River Audubon Center, in Southbury, Connecticut. "I'm collecting data from this property on lepidoptera [butterflies and moths] and handing it to the DEP for their atlas. I gave the teenager a net, showed him the techniques and he went out to catch them. I just didn't have the energy to sprint off in the meadow chasing a butterfly, whereas he had endless amounts of energy. He would run off, catch it, and bring it back to me. I'd make the photograph and the identification and send it off. He not only learned a lot about butterflies, he also had a good time."

Maybe you would like to volunteer "in the field" by serving on the water. The Hudson River sloop *Clearwater* accepts volunteer crew members at least 16 years old for one-week cruises. What do you do aboard ship? As the sloop navigates the Hudson River, New York Harbor and Long Island Sound, you may take the helm or help manage the sails. With crowds of children and adults aboard at each stop, you may also be asked to answer questions and explain the *Clearwater*'s mission of increasing public awareness of how an estuary works. Your duties can range from taking elementary school children through simple tests of water chemistry to reviewing how the *Clearwater* program, over 25 years, has saved the Hudson River ecosystem from environmental death.

(Courtesy: Hudson River sloop *Clearwater*)

The program built around the Hudson River sloop Clearwater *has helped save the river's ecosystem from environmental hazards for two decades. Located in Poughkeepsie, New York, the group welcomes volunteer crew members who are at least 16 years old.*

ABOARD THE *CLEARWATER*

Eleventh-grader Arielle Soloff lived aboard the *Clearwater* as a teen volunteer for a week during the summer of 1997. Ask her what she did and you may think it would be simpler to ask her what she *didn't* do. Her answer: "We had two kinds of sails, or cruises—education sails and member sails. The volunteers were responsible for teaching the day campers who came aboard. There were five stations that the campers go to. They are fish, plankton, navigation, main cabin and chemistry. As a volunteer student, you had to teach main cabin and navigation, but you could teach all five if you wanted to, and I taught all five. They're each 15 minutes, and you go around with a group of the camp kids and teach them about it.

"And then I helped with sailing and raising the mast and cleaning the boat—stuff like that. At night you talk with the members and help with the sails. And of course we had the daily chores—helping the cook, cleaning the main cabin, cleaning toilets, washing dishes and other jobs. We had deck wash every morning. And every morning we had workshops, like the physics of sailing, and how to throw dock lines and do other things on the boat. And preserving the environment."

TEACHING

You can teach about the environment. In the SSC, experienced volunteers, often before they reach college, regularly teach younger students about the connection between consumerism and environmentalism—what the things we buy are made of and why it is important to buy recyclables. Or you might teach them how to run a press conference or a lobbying program, how to recruit other students, how to make teamwork effective or how to run a successful meeting. All these have been subjects of workshops presented by older students to younger members of the SSC.

Rachel Jones, a Kids F.A.C.E. volunteer who just finished ninth grade, taught recycling for two years. She made presentations to third- and fourth-graders. "First I told them about how the club got started and helped make them aware of what is going on in the world," she says. "Then I talked about recycling and did activities with them. For instance, I set up a big box with all kinds of recyclable materials inside. At the other end of the classroom, I put up a recycling booth. The students formed teams and did a relay race. They had to run and sort out all the recycling—the clear glass, the green glass, the different plastics with the codes stamped on the bottoms. This activity taught them about the different types of recyclables and many kids actually began separating out the items at home."

How did Rachel get excused from her own classes to go teach younger kids? "The school I'm at is pretty flexible," she says, "because they're impressed with Kids F.A.C.E. So they let me go as long as I made up my work."

Mostly I do a lot of public speaking, making people aware of the whole situation with the environment and Kids F.A.C.E. Sometimes I'll know people at the school and they'll be interested in having me come to their classrooms, but a lot of the time I have to call and ask. So it just kind of works out.

> —Rachel Jones, high school sophomore,
> Kids F.A.C.E., Nashville, Tennessee

(Courtesy: The Nature Conservancy, Middletown, CT)

Sam Willis, a volunteer for The Nature Conservancy in Connecticut, sets up a one-meter square to be used at an archaeological dig at Devil's Den Preserve in Weston, Connecticut. Sam is also a trained natural history guide who leads program walks for the public.

Suppose you are teaching the elderly about recycling, like the West Haven, Connecticut, teenagers have done. To be an effective teacher, you will become knowledgeable about how not all plastics, glass or metals are the same. You will learn how to explain why certain types must be carefully sorted from others, and why plastic bags and worn-out dishpans are sometimes unwelcome at drop-off centers because they could last up to 400 years in the landfill.

Another helpful and interesting job is at a nature center that offers a day camp for younger kids during the summer. "Our teen volunteers are a big help with our day program," says Susan Quincy, coordinator of teen volunteers at the Flanders Nature Center in Woodbury, Connecticut. "It's for children ages 4 through 12. They help with the kids' activities on the trails, and they usually know most of the games. Most of our teen volunteers have been here at the camp or involved with the nature center programs for years, so they're very good—you can turn around and give them the name of a game and they can explain the rules and then lead the kids in the game—whereas our summer staff, which are teachers, rotate through, so we may have the same person who was here last year, but not always. So our teen volunteers give us something to fall back on."

THE SMALLEST THING MAKES A DIFFERENCE

"We went around to every class and gave presentations about the environment and ways kids can make a difference in the environment," says Jennings Smith, a ninth-grader who is North Carolina state representative in Kids F.A.C.E. "That's the main goal, to let kids know they can make a difference in the environment. A lot of kids don't know that there is something they can do, even if it's just planting a tree or something like that. That helps clean the air. The smallest thing makes a difference, and that's what we try to get across to them."

TEENS TEACHING TEENS

"Today we had a group that focused on the organic aspect of the food chain and where our food comes from," says Susan Quincy, coordinator of teen volunteers, Flanders Nature Center in Woodbury, Connecticut. "I had two people do the program with me. One is in college and the other is a senior in high school. They have been volunteers for a couple of years. Now they're able to actually lead the program and teach—and this was a large group, two classes of 35 kids each.

"They've been involved with all the educational programs—endangered species, soil science, the metamorphosis cycle, the food web, keeping water clean—so they have a broad knowledge. It's wonderful because they can pass on what they learned here to the next crew of kids."

CHAPTER THREE

You Can Do What These Three Teens Did

*M*eet three teenagers who have been active for a long time in helping to protect the environment. They have accomplished what seemed to adults to be near miracles. Each has earned major recognition for his or her work.

WHAT DAVE DID

Early in 1996, during his junior year in high school, Dave Karpf heard that the Belt Woods in Maryland, near the District of Columbia border, were to be destroyed to make way for a housing development. "This was the last old-growth forest in the mid-Atlantic plain," he says, "and also the home of the highest density of migratory songbirds."

Dave organized a drive for petitions in his county's schools and took 1,000 signatures to the state capitol in Annapolis. "We did a lot of work, from lobbying and letter writing to testifying in hearings," he notes. "The woods were saved."

From that beginning, Dave organized the Montgomery County Student Environmental Activists (MCSEA). It soon became an arm of the Sierra Student Coalition. In October 1996, a week before election day, Dave had a call from Larry Bowen, the conservation chairperson of the Sierra Club. "He told us about a bad bill that had been passed by the general assembly," says Dave. "We already knew about it. It was going to make it voluntary instead of mandatory for people to get their cars tested for emissions. We were trying to get the governor to veto it. Larry asked, 'Can you guys get a few hundred petition signatures together over the next 48 hours?'

"I told him we could do a lot more than that. And he said that between MCSEA and a group up in Baltimore, if we could get a thousand signatures together, we could really make it part of the campaign.

"We talked to the Baltimore people and we wound up getting 2,000 petition signatures in less than two school days. Our efforts shut down the governor's fax machine for two days!" The governor vetoed the bill.

The idea behind MCSEA, explains Dave, "is that there are a lot of students who have strong feelings for the earth and want to make a difference but have no idea how to get involved. Before I knew about Belt Woods and other things, I thought if I want to help the earth, I can recycle, and if I want to take big steps, well, I can help start a recycling program in my school or make it better. But there's so much more to do and people don't know that. When I talk to kids, their eyes just light up and they say, 'Wow, you can get stuff done, you can really make a difference.' We now have 70 members from 10 or 12 different high schools. We work with the Sierra Club and local groups, and we work with other student groups around the nation through the Sierra Student Coalition. And we have a very good time doing it."

WHAT TARA DID

In 1988, when Tara Church was eight years old, she and her Brownie troop used paper plates during a camping trip—then regretted using them. Tara proposed planting a tree as penance.

(Courtesy: Gail Church/Tree Musketeers, El Segundo, CA)

On behalf of the youth directors of Tree Musketeers, founder Tara Church accepts the President's Volunteer Action Award from President Clinton in a Rose Garden ceremony on Earth Day 1994.

49

One tree led to another, and the trees led Tara to found Tree Musketeers, a nonprofit environmental group run by kids.

Tara lives in El Segundo, California. "It's a very small town," she says, "surrounded on all sides by pollution—the Los Angeles airport, the Chevron oil refinery and a sewage plant. We're sort of immersed in pollution."

Over a decade, while that first tree—a sycamore sapling—grew 40 feet tall, Tara led Tree Musketeers to a host of accomplishments:

- Some 700 trees planted by youth as a green pollution barrier between El Segundo and the airport.
- The opening of her town's first recycling center in 1990. Tree Musketeers led the committee that wrote the town's waste management plan.
- The operation of a national environmental hotline and publication of a bimonthly magazine, *Grassroots Youth,* that has 60,000 readers.
- The creation of a National Environmental Youth Summit for 11- to 18-year-olds who are interested in reforestation and related issues. To get adult support and the money to launch the summit, Tara, then 12, pitched the idea to a conference room full of people who had influence in Washington, D.C. She also recruited 13 teams of teens and adults as planning partners and chaired their steering committee. With representatives from all 50 states and 35 foreign countries, the first summit was held in Cincinnati in 1993. A second, in 1995, drew 600 young people to Snowbird, Utah, from dozens of environmental groups around the United States. A third is planned for Los Angeles in the summer of 1998, with a crowd of 1,000 expected. With the summits run entirely by and for kids, "no adult can come without a youth partner," says Tara.

- The creation of the Memory Tree Program, in which people plant trees rather than sending flowers to commemorate the lives of loved ones.

Did doing all this mean that Tara led a one-track life? No. As she rose through junior high and high school, she was an honors student busy in many activities, a cheerleader and a homecoming princess. In recognition of her accomplishments, she even earned the prestigious Silver Award, the highest award a cadette Girl Scout can receive. In 1994, she was invited to the White House to receive the President's Volunteer Action Award from President Bill Clinton in a Rose Garden ceremony celebrating Earth Day.

By her senior year in high school, Tara found the University of Southern California recruiting her—"hot and heavy," as her mother later said. Despite the fact that she had been too busy to try to maintain a straight-A average, Tara received a full scholarship based on her record of accomplishment.

At the University of Southern California, Tara is majoring in political science and history, with a minor in French. Her goal? Not to be an environmental engineer but to pursue environmental issues in the political arena. In May 1997, she capped her teen career when she was one of only 50 representatives of nonprofit organizations nationwide invited to participate in the president's Summit for America's Future in Philadelphia.

Tara continues to encourage teenagers—and younger children—to get involved in volunteer environmental activities and to believe they can make a difference. "I'm not a pessimist," she says, "but I know that environmental crises are everywhere, and if we don't take action, there won't be much of a planet left. I want there to be a great quality of life for my kids and for their kids' kids. I've encountered people who didn't have faith in the capabilities of a young girl. I was never shunned, but I realized that people were humoring me, saying things like, 'Oh, how cute! The kids want to plant trees.'

"But I was able to recognize that, no matter what other people said, we young people can accomplish things. With us, there's excitement. There's fire, there's passion. Youth activism not only empowers each kid but introduces impressive results for society as a whole."

We young people can accomplish things. With us, there's excitement. There's fire, there's passion.

WHAT MELISSA DID

In Nashville, Tennessee, in 1989, when Melissa Poe was nine, she saw a television show in which an angel (played by Michael Landon) advised that our water and air could become so polluted that the human race might die if we failed to protect the environment. "It's not too late," said the angel. "People who care will do something."

Melissa cared. She wrote a letter to President George Bush.

The reply from the White House was a form letter about drug abuse. But within three months Melissa had written to local newspapers, TV stations and politicians with ideas on controlling pollution. Her voice was heard on talk radio. She phoned an advertising firm and induced them to mount her letter to the president on a billboard in Nashville. Then, realizing that the president might not see it there, she got the advertising firm to display it on Washington's Pennsylvania Avenue near the White House. Next, in April 1990, the Outdoor Advertising Association of America put her letter on 250 billboards around the United States, with at least one in every state.

Melissa's address was on many of the billboards. People wrote to her. She formed a club called Kids F.A.C.E. (Kids For A Clean Environment).

"In the beginning," Melissa says, "it was just six of my friends. We did whatever we could—recycling, planting trees, little things to help."

> Dear Mr. President,
>   Please will you do something about pollution. I want to live till I am 100 years old.
>   Mr. President, if you ignore this letter we will all die of pollution and the ozone layer.
>   Please Help,
>   Melissa Poe, Age 9

(Courtesy: Kids F.A.C.E., Nashville, TN)

When Melissa Poe sent this letter to President George Bush in 1989, it was the beginning of a club called Kids F.A.C.E. (Kids For A Clean Environment). The group was started by seven friends and now has more than 300,000 members.

But the *Today* show invited Melissa to appear and talk about how people can help stop pollution. Immediately, the Kids F.A.C.E. club went national. By 1997, it had 3,000 chapters in 15 countries, with some 300,000 members. Under Melissa's leadership the group has accomplished many things, including:

- Free membership to children and teachers who want to get involved in their communities. Costs are paid by donations from corporations and individual adults.

(Courtesy: Kids F.A.C.E., Nashville, TN)

Fifteen-year-old Melissa Poe (right) and Rachel Jones at the Earth Flag Booth on the Mall in Washington, D.C., at the 25th Earth Day celebration in April 1995. The Kids Earth Flag is in the background.

- A telephone hot-line (800-952-3223) from which you can get material on membership and request environmental information for your school reports and projects.
- The newsletter *Kids F.A.C.E. Illustrated,* sent free to members and schools. It is loaded with ideas and how-to's, and it reports on successful youth projects and other news about the environment.
- The Kids' Earth Flag, a banner 200 feet long by 100 feet wide that was handcrafted by members who sent in 20,000 individual squares. Sewn by volunteers into 50- by 50-foot

sections, the flag was unveiled on the Mall in Washington to celebrate the 25th anniversary of Earth Day in 1995. Since then, it has toured the nation's schools and communities on a "Journey of Hope." Local chapters of Kids F.A.C.E. continue to make more sections for it.

- The School of Trees, an awareness program that establishes the importance of planting trees in urban areas and tells you how to plant them.
- Kids' Yard, a program that offers guidelines on setting up outdoor wildlife habitats in your own backyard, school yard or neighborhood.
- Youth Environmental Summit, in which Kids F.A.C.E. was a cosponsor, with Tree Musketeers and others, of the five-day event. Eighteen teens and adults developed and presented the bulk of the summit's workshops.
- A special animal-care team of teens who work to increase awareness of endangered animals and raise money to provide food and medicine for injured marine mammals.
- A youth leadership program in which teenagers who serve on the national governing board of Kids F.A.C.E. visit schools around the country to make oral presentations on the power of the individual and believing in yourself.
- The "Power of One" campaign, designed to help you become an active participant in your community by doing service projects. It includes a videocassette and radio public-service announcements recorded by Nashville teen members of Kids F.A.C.E. along with country-music artists.

Did heading up all this activity affect Melissa's "regular" life? At 16, she considered herself "pretty normal." She swam and ran cross-country on her high school teams and served on the student council. At 17, she realized it was time to pass responsibility as CEO (Child Executive Officer) of Kids F.A.C.E. to a younger person. The organization's 1997 election resulted in a tie. Ashley Craw, 14, of Nashville, Tennessee, and Rachel Jones, 15, of Bowling Green, Kentucky, were elected to succeed Melissa.

"When someone says, 'You're just a kid, you can't do that,' I want to prove them wrong," says Melissa. "I tell kids that they can do something. They can get involved and start a club or do something at their school. Don't let anyone tell you that you can't do what you want. As long as you believe that you can make a difference, you can do it."

CHAPTER FOUR

What It Takes to Help Protect the Environment

Working to help protect the environment will provide you with exciting and challenging experiences. It will, however, require a lot of hard work to get good things done. As a teen volunteer, certain things will be required of you. These include:

- commitment and attitude,
- basic skills and training, and
- strength and stamina.

COMMITMENT AND ATTITUDE

As in any work you volunteer for, the people you work with will expect dependability more than anything else. They rely on you to be there when you say you'll be there and do what you say you'll do. Your commitment is what counts.

What makes you dependable is your own interest in the work. Are you concerned about the environment? Are you thinking of becoming a biologist? A naturalist of any kind? Does the whole field of natural science appeal to you? Your interest in such subjects will affect your commitment to helping protect our planet for future generations and to teaching others the importance of protecting it.

Beth Gardner, director of the Sierra Club's Inner City Outings program in Seattle, Washington, discusses what commitment is all about. "Most of the kids that we're accepting as youth leaders have been

(Courtesy: Paul Fusco/DEP Wildlife Division, State of CT)

If you plan to study natural sciences, volunteering for an environmental organization may help your future career. These teenagers attempt to catch turtles for a diamondback terrapin survey conducted by the Wildlife Division of the Connecticut Department of Environmental Protection.

pretty regularly involved going on our trips," she says. "We've handpicked them after they've been active not only on trips but doing other things that we do as a group, such as fund-raising. Basically, they have to show commitment, they have to show interest. We're not going to just take some kid off the street who says, 'Oh, I want to work with you.' "

Your commitment means time. Dave Karpf, teen founder of Montgomery County Student Environmental Activists (MCSEA) in Maryland, explains: "For someone who wants to get involved in an organization like this, it'll be a great experience if you make it so. If you commit yourself, you will love it. It will take time out of your day and you'll find a lot less time to spend with your friends and your family and doing schoolwork. But you'll enjoy what you're doing."

SATISFACTION AT MANY LEVELS

"I grew up in Washington, D.C., and saw the development right in my backyard," says Malka Fenyvesi, a teen volunteer at the Sierra Student Coalition. "I saw the pollution, waste management and sprawl right there. In every respect, it impacts you and your family and your world."

Malka believes that joining an environmental group is a great experience. It allows you to meet and get involved with new people and to learn group skills. "I've made most of my friends through it. So I would say, get involved," says Malka.

It's all a matter of your attitude. If you want to help our environment survive through the 21st century and beyond, you cannot be shy about it. You have to bring an attitude of enthusiasm to the work. And you have to be able to envision the long-range effect of what you are doing. Laura Mason, who volunteered with Seattle's Inner City Outings through her senior year in high school in 1997, says, "I've spent a lot of time in the outdoors, and I wanted to share my experiences as a volunteer. But I don't have any special area. My

(Courtesy: The Nature Conservancy, Middletown, CT)

If you want to help protect the environment, consider volunteering for a nature conservancy. Jamie Marion, a trained natural history guide for The Nature Conservancy in Connecticut, also does field work for the group. Pictured above, Jamie sifts soil at an archaeological dig at the Devil's Den Preserve in Weston, Connecticut.

background is backpacking." Laura understood that her enthusiasm for getting younger kids out of the inner city on weekends would give them a long-term awareness of the natural environment.

There are times when you're tired, when you'd just like to stay in bed and sleep instead of getting up at 7:30 on a Saturday morning to take a bunch of kids on an outing. But you do it because it has to be on weekends. Everyone works or goes to school on weekdays.

—Teen volunteer Laura Mason,
Sierra Club Inner City Outings,
Seattle, Washington

Of course, you may have a strong interest in nature and the environment. Sara Colangelo, who spent the summer before her senior year in high school volunteering at the Connecticut headquarters of The Nature Conservancy, says, "I plan to major in biology in college. I had taken an honors biology course and really loved the subject. I read about volunteers in The Nature Conservancy magazine, and so I called there to see if they needed anyone.

"It is a lot of work," continues Sara. "I've had people say, 'Why are you working there seven hours a day? You need to be making money.' But it's something I really like to do. And it's nice to see what I might be doing with my life later on."

BASIC SKILLS AND TRAINING

The most valuable skills you can bring to protecting the environment are "people skills"—the ability to get along with others, understand their points of view, and put across your point of view on the issues.

The ability to get on your feet and speak to a group is also important. Not everyone who works in the environmental area has to be a good public speaker, but if you have this skill—or can work on gaining it—you will have an advantage. When Rachel Jones was running for the office of CEO (Child Executive Officer) of Kids F.A.C.E. in the summer before 10th grade, she said, "I was getting training for public speaking through the Girl Scouts, when I was 10. That's when I heard about Kids F.A.C.E. And my public speaking got me involved in it."

Rachel represented Kids F.A.C.E. at the first national environmental summit conference put on by Tree Musketeers. "After that one in Cincinnati," she says candidly, "I started my own. A girl who was in the club with me and I co-coordinated a Southern Regional Environmental Summit the next year, because we had gotten kind of inspired when we went to Cincinnati. And then the next year we went to Utah to the second national. And I represented Kids F.A.C.E. at an Urban Forestry Conference in Minnesota."

Other useful skills? Every organization needs help in the day-to-day work in the office: typing, filing, data entry in the computer. If you are comfortable handling telephone calls—speak clearly, explain carefully, and listen alertly—you offer a skill that not everyone brings to the office.

Every organization needs help in the day-to-day work in the office.

STRENGTH AND STAMINA

Many volunteer positions entail long hours and have you on your feet all day. In general, you should be healthy and energetic, but there is something for everyone. You can usually tailor your duties and hours to fit your personal needs.

How old do you have to be? You'll run into very few age limits. As you've already read in this book, not only teenagers but also many thousands of elementary school kids are active in environmental groups.

THAT LIMBO AGE

"In our educational facilities, we do a lot of programs," says Susan Quincy, coordinator of teen volunteers at the Flanders Nature Center in Woodbury, Connecticut, "but they're for kids just up to the age of twelve. And then there's a huge gap. You have a group of young teens who are thirteen to fifteen who do not have anything to do during the summer months. We're a rural area—no movies, no fast food. So they're basically sitting home and they get bored. No programs are geared toward them. They're getting too old to hang out in parks and recreation, they don't want to go to day camps anymore—they're at that limbo age. So the age we work with are generally thirteen to fifteen. And as they get older, we can use them to present our programs for the younger kids."

Chapter Five
What's in It for You?

*L*ike other volunteer work, helping to protect the earth is an interesting way to meet your community service requirements, if your school demands such service. It gives you the joy of helping the environment and working with others toward a common goal.

It offers many other benefits as well. It helps you toward your future career. And even if you do not become a biologist, naturalist or activist, you gain practical knowledge you can use throughout your life.

CAREER BENEFITS

If you're thinking about a future in biology, forestry, botany, zoology or any other field related to nature and the environment, this kind of volunteering will be helpful. Maybe you're like the ninth-grade youth leader described by Beth Gardner, director of the Sierra Club's Inner City Outings (ICO) in Seattle. "She started with us as a participant in outings six years ago and is really interested in environmental education as a career," reports Gardner. "She's done lots of things for our group. She made a videotape on why bats are great. They use it at the local zoo. She's going to the national ICO conference and will probably be the only youth leader there from all over the country. She's actively exploring careers in environmental education."

Helping to protect the environment can give you a chance to explore many specialized fields. The more you learn about them as a volunteer, the more your interest in a career may be stimulated. Here are some examples:

- *Forestry.* Your career interest could be *silviculture,* the science of growing trees—or perhaps fire protection, control of insects and diseases, the harvesting of timber or the management of watersheds.
- *Wildlife biology.* Your work could be in nature and forest reserves, rangelands, fish hatcheries or wildlife refuges. It would include preparing environmental impact studies.

I hope to get a job in an environmental organization. I've devoted so much time to environmental programs and I love the work so much that it's the only thing I can imagine really enjoying.

—Teen founder Dave Karpf,
Montgomery County
Student Environmental Activists
(MCSEA), Maryland

- *Soil conservation.* Your job would be the wise management of our resources in water, soil and plants. You could become an expert in such fields of agriculture as soil physics, range ecology and agronomy—the production of field crops.
- *Urban planning.* Cities and metropolitan areas need environmental experts to help plan growth and improve public services such as recycling and waste management.
- *Other sciences.* As a civil engineer, geologist or expert in waste disposal or air and water pollution, you could be a valuable contributor to the conservation of the environment.

One benefit that will help you in any future career is that many environmental protection activities teach you about leadership—how to make things happen. Tree Musketeers, for example, offers a Leadership Education and Action Program (LEAP) that trains younger teens by showing them how to manage three-month projects. At the Flanders Nature Center in Woodbury, Connecticut, Susan Quincy, coordinator of teen volunteers, says, "We run a June training session for kids 13 to 15 years old. They get to take on a leadership role. During the one-week, half-day sessions, the participants learn the technical aspects of handling the animals themselves, checking the animals for injuries, and what to report to the staff. They learn how to walk the trails and work with a group. They are trained to work with children and to help the youngsters but not do things for them. They learn how to keep observing and making sure nobody gets lost or tags too far behind. It gives them work experience and a leadership role.

Many environmental protection activities teach you about leadership—how to make things happen.

"One thing more," adds Quincy. "We get calls from young teens who say, 'My Mom said I have to find something to do this summer, can I come out and volunteer? Or else I have to go to camp.' So we're the salvation for some teens. But they work out just as well, too, because they are motivated not to go to day camp."

WHAT ABOUT COLLEGE?

Will volunteering in environmental protection help you get into college? Dave Karpf, teen founder of MCSEA, shares his insight: "During my interview at Oberlin College, the admissions officer looked at my folder and then looked at me. After a moment she said, 'You're the guy who saved the woods.'" Dave entered Oberlin in the fall of 1997.

The point is: Colleges grab people who get good things done.

(Courtesy: Kids F.A.C.E., Nashville, TN)

Organizing events that will capture media attention is important. At Earth Day 1995, held in Washington, D.C., Kids F.A.C.E. group founder Melissa Poe speaks at the awards ceremony.

YOU BECOME AWARE . . .
AND MAKE PEOPLE AWARE

What's in it for you is *awareness*—in two ways. You become aware of environmental needs and issues, and you help to make others aware of them. That's what leadership is all about.

Your awareness in both senses becomes heightened as you find out more and more about the problems our environment faces today. Here is how high school junior Alexis Goldstein describes the feeling: "I've always been interested in the environment, always wanted to protect it ever since I was a kid. I always felt really almost connected to nature and all that and the idea that everything is connected. I didn't really know too much about how much we were hurting the earth, but I always felt threatened by any effort to destroy what we have. So it made me really upset when I heard about all the destruction that was going on in the rain forest and that kind of thing. And the more I learned about it, the more I felt obligated to do something about it. I felt so horrible that I was just sitting idly by. And I thought, what else can I do, what else is there to do? Then I went to a meeting and saw all that you can do and I was overwhelmed."

LEADERS ARE ALSO STUDENTS

"One of the unique things about the Sierra Student Coalition," says Sage Rockermann, president of the group, "is that it's not just a lot of students who volunteered. Our program is entirely *run* by the students.

"All of our leaders, all of the people who are calling the shots and asking the students to volunteer their time, are also students. But they've been around a little bit longer in leadership positions. Most of them started out volunteering just a couple of years ago and got more involved."

To become aware and make others aware, your work with environmental groups and projects will take you into the real world beyond school, a world in which you write letters, deliver speeches, and meet people in business, in government agencies, and in politics. Its a world in which, while still a student, you learn how to network with old and new friends at receptions and conferences.

What other specific skills are in it for you? Let's look at the Sierra Student Coalition (SSC) for examples of other kinds of valuable knowledge and skills you can get from working with environmental protection groups:

- *Fund-raising.* Or, as SSC puts it, "fun-draising." You find out why bake sales and car washes are not good ideas. You learn how to narrow down suggestions to the most practical, where to begin your drive, what kinds of causes people are most likely to support, how to reach many goals with a single event.

- *Lobbying.* Here you learn what homework to do before you lobby, what materials to take along, how to line up what you want to say and keep it simple. You also learn when to "close the sale" and leave.

- *Meetings.* Running a meeting is a skill you can learn. You'll discover how to prepare an agenda, what materials to supply, why it's important to get people involved immediately, what to do after the meeting.

- *Recruiting.* Every organization needs a steady stream of new people. In learning recruiting, you find out what motivates others to volunteer, where you can find likely recruits, how to make newcomers feel they belong.

- *Media.* In learning to handle press relations, you discover why the media need you as much as you need them, what to put into a press release, when to call a press conference

69

(and when not to), what key ingredient makes the basis of good press relations.

WORKING WITH THE MEDIA

Alexis Goldstein, of the Maryland Sierra Student Coalition, picked up valuable communications skills when her group wanted to stage a boycott of Shell gasoline stations after world news reports alleged that Shell Oil was polluting the air and farmland of Nigeria.

"None of us had ever done anything with the media before," the 10th-grader says, "but one of the older activists told me how to do a media advisory and a press release. Then I made the media calls. It was a good experience for me. Now I know how to do it. Before that incident, I didn't even know you needed to contact the media."

CHAPTER SIX
Is It Right for You?

*Y*ou've been considering some of the areas for protecting the environment in which you might volunteer. You've thought about what you'd be doing, and now you have an idea of what's in it for you.

The next question that comes up is: Is it *right* for you? To answer that one, you have to compare the good and bad sides—the advantages and satisfactions that you can get from volunteering to help protect the environment and the disadvantages and dissatisfactions you may have to face. When you have reviewed some of these, you can take a self-quiz to determine if this area is right for you.

ADVANTAGES AND SATISFACTIONS

Working with people in the environmental area helps you find out whether you want to concentrate on this field when you get to college and later in your lifework. If you are thinking, but not sure about, being a biologist, botanist, forester, farmer, conservationist or any kind of specialist in waste management or air and water pollution, you can find out before you make a commitment in terms of your education. Finding out can save you time and money.

Let's look at some of the advantages you gain:

- *Handling responsibility.* In most of the situations described in this book, you get good practice in taking on responsibility. As you succeed in handling it, you gain a second advantage: You improve your own self-image or self-esteem. You get to know your own capabilities and limitations.

- *Gaining recognition.* With your voluntary service, you make new friends not only among your peers but also among the adult volunteers and the staff people with whom you work. Getting their recognition and approval can be especially valuable. For example, they can help you when you need recommendations or references to put on college or job applications.

- *Making new friends.* Volunteering in an environmental activist group or in a nature center or land trust introduces you to new people beyond your usual group—those your own age, and others who are older or younger than you.

My friendships changed when I got into this. I found I had a lot more in common with the activists, and I liked spending more of my time with them and less with my school friends.

—High school sophomore Alexis Goldstein, Sierra Student Coalition, Maryland

- *Learning something new.* By the end of ninth grade in May 1997, Rachel Jones had several years' experience in Kids F.A.C.E. "But I always learn something new," she says. "I go on trips to environmental conferences and summits, and it seems like every time I go somewhere it just opens another door for me. I'll meet somebody else and do another project with another group, so it's always another opportunity."

(Courtesy: Gail Church/Tree Musketeers, El Segundo, CA)

Tree Musketeers, established in 1987 by eight-year-old Tara Church, began by helping fight pollution in El Segundo, California. Now, members plant trees, promote recycling programs and host a number of youth summits on the regional and national levels. (From left) Tree Musketeers founders Sabrina and Alisa Wise are helped by Angie McCall on Arbor Day 1994.

The satisfactions? Listen to some of the teenagers who are volunteering in environmental work:

"The way I look at it," says Jennings Smith of Kids F.A.C.E., "is that it's helping others. I'm one of those people who enjoy making presentations and speaking to the public. So that's satisfying. But I also think something needs to be done for the environment. If it's ruined, then our life is ruined. If we don't do something now, the problems are just going to grow worse and worse."

Tara Church, founder of Tree Musketeers, feels, "The work that we do is extremely rewarding. We're not only making a difference in the community and in the environment. We're making a difference in the lives of young people. When you give somebody leadership training and they get empowered and they learn to speak and actually give a speech in front of the city council for the first time, that's really exciting for me. And I know that in my eyes the environment is probably the most important issue that we need to focus on. It makes me very, very happy to be doing something for the planet."

"It makes me feel really good," says Rachel Jones of Kids F.A.C.E. "After I've done my speeches and projects and opened other people's eyes to something they've never seen before, I feel good because I know they're interested and they've learned something and usually had a good time. I've had so many opportunities to go to different parts of the country and meet with other kids who have the same interests. That's one of the best things, when you go to the summit, because you get to meet people from all over the world. They come from everywhere, and you just make new friends and you learn with other people. You always meet new people and you always have an opportunity to do different fun things."

"It's fulfilling for me," says Alexis Goldstein, of the Sierra Student Coalition. "All my work in environmentalism has shown me just how much you can make an impact, in anything. I had no idea you could go down to Congress and tell the legislators what you think. When I get back from a meeting, I just get this rush. It makes me feel really proud. It gives me a good idea of my own powers. Activism will definitely be a part of my life."

"I think it's great," says Sara Colangelo, a summer volunteer at the Connecticut Nature Conservancy, "for any student who's working in the classroom to see what people do in the real world. For my biology course I had written a paper on wetlands. Working here and seeing research being done firsthand shows me, with all the course work I've done in the past year, how it's pertinent to what people really do. I learn something new every day—literally."

Sara sees another advantage. "Basically, I'm controlling how long I work," she says. "I'm like a workaholic type of person. When I'm working on something, I like to do it all-out. I've worked maybe nine to five every day, but if I want to leave earlier, I control my own schedule. I'm going to start visiting colleges soon, so if I need to take a day off I'll take a day off, it's not a big deal. I think that if you're volunteering, the people you're volunteering for are generally understanding and respectful of your time. They respect the fact that you're volunteering, so if you need to leave early, it shouldn't be a problem."

"I wanted a way to volunteer my time that was also fun for me," says Laura Mason, high school senior with the Sierra Club's Inner City Outings in Seattle. "I've spent a lot of time with kids and I like kids, so it's rewarding for me just to see the kids having fun and learning about the environment. The area I live in is a suburb of Seattle, which is just so safe and so protected and I feel so fortunate that I just can't feel right about myself unless I help someone else who doesn't have all the advantages that I do. And it kind of gets me back in touch with myself, because I can get caught up in a lot of stuff and forget how nice it is to be outdoors."

ANY DISADVANTAGES?

Now the bad news. Here are the negatives you should think about:

- *No pay.* You must weigh the advantages you will get from a volunteer job against the disadvantage of giving up time that you could be using to earn money.

- *Social life.* If you make a commitment to be up early every Saturday to take inner-city children on an outing, your Friday nights may be cut short. If you are an ardent activist, your friends may not understand—as Alexis Goldstein learned. "It gave me a bad image with my other friends," she says. "You get an attitude—you want everyone to be an activist."

If you are an ardent activist, your friends may not understand.

There were kids at my school who were not so kind toward me when I started this. They wouldn't talk to me, or they would gang up on me and say, "Let's get her." Even today, kids come up to me and say, in a snide way, "Aren't you that save-the-world girl?"

—Kids F.A.C.E. founder Melissa Poe

- *It takes time.* Dave Karpf can tell you about that. "If you're going to become devoted," he says, "it's important to realize that it's a serious time commitment. I know people who have given up a sport in school because they've decided to devote themselves to MCSEA [Montgomery County Student Environmental Activists]. You have only so many hours in the day and you have to make your choices. I did well in school but, to be honest, I certainly could have done even better. But I found something that I loved and instead of taking fifteen extra minutes to study for that test, I called the membership to tell them about a meeting coming up."

- *Possible burnout.* "I guess the only downside of doing the activism is that you get burned out," says Alexis Goldstein, "because you're so overwhelmed sometimes. You keep hearing about these things that force you to open your eyes and look around, and it can be really frightening at times. You get to the point where you're so frustrated you have to stop and get away because it's so heavy."

SOME COMMENTS ON DISADVANTAGES

Several teen leaders were asked about possible disadvantages in volunteering with their organizations.

"I don't really feel that our work has any disadvantages," said Rachel Jones, copresident of Kids F.A.C.E., "because it's always fun and you can get more people involved. Sometimes you have to miss some things, when you go on trips, for example. But it's always your choice. It's not really like you're giving up anything."

"The only disadvantage I see," said Tara Church, founder of Tree Musketeers, "is that sometimes I think the world doesn't look at environmental issues as serious. They're not as compelling as homeless people or starving children. Sometimes I think the importance of the cause is not recognized as much as it needs to be."

Sierra Student Coalition director Sage Rockermann, who is slightly older and came up through the teen volunteer ranks, is realistic about the disadvantages. "You can't do everything, because volunteering is such a time commitment," she says. "You might not be able to play a sport or have time for certain hobbies. You see your friends less sometimes. I'm also friends with the people I work with here, but it's definitely a time commitment, so you need to balance things."

(Continued on page 78)

(Continued from page 77)

Dave Karpf, founder of Maryland's Montgomery County Student Environmental Activists (MCSEA), sees some disadvantages that turn out to be advantages. "It really depends how far you get into it," he says. "If I wasn't the leader of MCSEA, I probably would have a paid job. But just as a plain volunteer, you don't have to give that up. Most members have paying jobs. It doesn't stop that. The main thing you lose is time you would spend with other friends in a social setting. But the positive side of that, which a lot of us have found, is that many of us are now the closest of friends. As you get more into it, you start finding a shift in the people you hang out with. I remember for myself, I had a group of friends and we'd all go over to someone's house and play cards or watch TV. Then as MCSEA progressed I started hanging out with these people who shared this common passion with me and instead we'd go have coffee somewhere and have a thoughtful discussion or we'd just go and play frisbee or something. You end up giving up very little."

GIVE YOURSELF A QUIZ

How do you know you're right for the job? Ask yourself some questions. Think before you answer.

- Can you commit anywhere from 30 to 200 hours of the school year, or 50 hours of your summer, to this work?
- Can you balance your schoolwork, a paying job and this volunteer job without "spreading yourself too thin"?
- Are you really concerned about the environment?
- Can you speak to a classroom or assembly of schoolmates?

(Courtesy: S.C. Delaney/U.S. Environmental Protection Agency)

These young children are already learning about recycling and how important it is in our society today.

- Are you an organizer? A leader?
- Can you face the fact that many people don't consider environmental issues to be as serious a problem as you may?
- Can you put up with teasing from peers who fail to understand your concern?
- Can you ask questions? When you don't understand, are you willing to say you don't understand?

• Are you willing to work in an office, doing the necessary "support work" that helps keep an environmentalist group or nature preserve going, rather than being in the field?

DO SOMETHING YOU REALLY ENJOY

"My advice to anyone who's thinking about volunteering for anything," says Sara Colangelo, teen volunteer at the Connecticut Nature Conservancy in Middletown, "would be, Think about what you want to do perhaps with your life, or not even thinking that far ahead, about something you really enjoy doing. I really love to be outside, and I'm very passionate about the environment. I really love to help the environment any way I can. So I decided to take something where I felt I would be giving up my time but also be getting a lot in return. If you're doing something you love to do, you'll happily volunteer for that, happily give your time.

"I have a friend who wants to be a doctor, so he's gone to Massachusetts General Hospital every Saturday of his life for three years, volunteering three hours a day there, because that's where he wants to be. It doesn't necessarily have to be what you want to do with your life, but do something you really enjoy."

CHAPTER SEVEN

Where to Find Opportunities

Start your search by checking with guidance counselors at your school and with the reference librarian in your public library. Ask about local branches or chapters of major organizations (see below), and about nearby arboretums, nature preserves and land trusts. See if a specific Nature Conservancy is near.

Put your phone book to work. In the Yellow Pages, check *Nature Centers.* Under *Chambers of Commerce,* find your community's C of C and call them to get the phone numbers of land trust leaders (usually home phone numbers, for most land trusts do not have enough money to maintain offices). Call your mayor's office for a list of non-profit organizations that welcome volunteers; check it out for environmentalist groups.

Each state has its Department of Environmental Protection (DEP). Check the heading under your state's name in the blue pages in your phone book, but don't be confused by the fact that the phone company insists on listing it as Environmental Protection Department and positions it under E rather than D. Call the DEP to find out what's near you.

Every state has wildlife rehabilitation, and they're always looking for volunteer help, especially in the spring when they have lots of birds that fall out of nests and other things that need help. So a teenager can make up mushes and feed them with eyedroppers and help clean out cages and do that kind of thing and is greatly appreciated.

—Susan Hageman, director, Environmental Education,
Southern Connecticut State University, New Haven

If you're stymied, contact such national organizations as these:

Hudson River Sloop *Clearwater,* Inc.
112 Market Street
Poughkeepsie, NY 12601
(914) 454-7673

Kids F.A.C.E.
P.O. Box 158254
Nashville, TN 37215
(615) 331-7381
(800) 952-3223;

National Wildlife Federation
8925 Leesburg Pike
Vienna, VA 22184-0001
(703) 790-4000
http://www.nwf.org

The Nature Conservancy
If you are interested in volunteering, The Conservancy requests that you contact its local chapters, which can direct you to conser-

vancies or land trusts near you. For phone numbers of offices in every state, see the Appendix.

River Network
P.O. Box 8787
Portland, OR 97207-8787
(503) 241-3506; fax (503) 241-9256
(800) 423-6747;

Sierra Club
85 Second Street, Second Floor
San Francisco, CA 94105-3441
(415) 977-5508; fax (415) 977-5799

Sierra Student Coalition (SSC)
P.O. Box 2402
Providence, RI 02906
(401) 861-6012; fax (401) 861-6241
www.ssc.org
Your membership in the SSC is registered automatically if you check "student" on any regular Sierra Club brochure or application.

Tree Musketeers
136 Main Street
El Segundo, CA 90245
(310) 322-0263; fax (310) 322-4482

What do you say when you call? Ask for the person who coordinates volunteers. You may not get that person on the first call, because all coordinators are busy and overworked. Be sure to leave a message, with your name and phone number, saying you want to find out about volunteering. Ask if you need an application form and if the coordinator can mail you one. Or you may offer to stop by and pick up the form.

If no one calls back within a few days, call again. Do not get discouraged. Persistence pays off. If you have decided on a particular place where you want to volunteer, keep at it. You may find that they accept applications only at certain times or seasons of the year.

Do not get discouraged. Persistence pays off.

If you can't get in right away, ask if they have a waiting list, and say you want to be put on it. Be sure to write thank-you letters that follow up on your calls. While you're thinking of them, you want *them* to be thinking of *you*.

What's the best age to start volunteering? I'd say when you're in middle school. That's usually the group we focus on if we want to do recruiting, because the kids are still young enough at that point to be open and to be affected by issues. Also, they generally have more time to care. If you start the process of doing good for society at a young age, it usually becomes embedded in the consciousness of that person and becomes a lifestyle.

—Tara Church, founder, Tree Musketeers

YOUR INTERVIEW

When you are interviewed, feel free to ask questions. What kind of training program will you have to go through? How many training meetings a week, for how many weeks? How many teen volunteers are in the program? Is there a period of probation, and how long is it?

Let your interviewer know that you have thought about your commitment to volunteering. Make him or her aware that you want to know what you are getting into in the same sense that he or she wants to know about you.

GET A RÉSUMÉ READY

Looking for a volunteer job is like looking for a paying job. You want to make the best possible impression. Handing a résumé to your interviewer makes two points:

1. That you have been somewhere and done something, and
2. That you know how to think about where you have been and what you have done.

What goes into your résumé? Your full name, address, age, grade in school, and school activities (e.g., Key Club, drama club, sports teams, science club, 4-H Club, publications). Stress any environment-related activities—in school or in your neighborhood or the larger community. And be sure to include part-time jobs, from baby-sitting to delivering newspapers to mowing lawns and shoveling snow. You want the reader of your résumé to see how well rounded you are.

HOW DO YOU LOOK?

Somebody said, "You get only one chance to make a good first impression." Dress for it, in clean, freshly pressed clothing. Make sure your hands and fingernails are clean. Shampoo. If you have short hair, it should be trimmed and well combed. If you have long hair, wear it in a braid or ponytail. Make it clear you know you shouldn't come to work with your hair flying in the breeze.

FOLLOW YOUR INCLINATION

"You've really got to go out and get it yourself," says Kate Sands, high school senior and volunteer at a Nature Conservancy in Connecticut. "And let your parents push you. I wanted to do something—go out

(Continued on page 86)

(Continued from page 85)

and clear a trail or something—and my Mom was saying, 'Well, call somebody, do this, call The Nature Conservancy,' until I finally did, and they said they would like someone to do some office work for them, and if a project came up I could work on it. And I thought it would be fun.

"They had some work parties, and I got familiar with some of the nature preserves, and it actually worked out well. I'm really glad she did make me. It's not always complete self-motivation. So I'd say, let yourself be pushed into a few things, because they'll really be fun for you. If you just have a slight inclination, follow it and see what comes up, even though some things might not pan out at all. But some things will and you'll have a lot of fun."

GLOSSARY

Agriculture. The science or art of farming.

Estuary. A body of water, partly surrounded by land, where fresh and salt water mix, such as the lower Hudson River or Long Island Sound.

Lepidoptera. The family of insects that are caterpillars as larvae.

Lobby. To conduct activities with the goal of influencing the opinions and/or votes of members of a legislative body.

Metamorphosis. A marked change in the physical form of an animal, as from caterpillar to butterfly or from tadpole to frog.

Steering committee. A committee that determines the order in which business will be discussed.

SUGGESTIONS FOR FURTHER READING

Some of the following books may be in the Young Adult or Juvenile section of your library. Don't be put off because they are "children's books." They offer good descriptions with plenty of detail.

Batten, Mary. *Nature's Tricksters: Animals and Plants That Aren't What They Seem.* San Francisco: Sierra Club, 1992.

Bell, Peter R. *Green Plants: Their Origin and Diversity.* Portland, OR: Timber, 1992.

Blashfield, Jean F., and W.B. Black. *Recycling.* Chicago: Children's Press, 1991.

Bleifield, Maurice. *Botany Projects for Young Scientists.* New York: Watts, 1992.

Burnie, David. *Plant.* New York: Knopf, 1989.

Cichonski, Thomas J., and Karen Hill, eds. *Recycling Sourcebook.* Detroit: Gale Research, 1993.

Dolan, Edward. *Our Poisoned Sky.* New York: Cobblehill, 1991.

Elsom, Derek M. *Atmospheric Pollution: Causes, Effects and Control Policies.* Oxford, England: Basil Blackwell, 1987.

Fustec, Fabienne. *Plants.* New York: Random House, 1993.

Gay, Kathlyn. *Caretakers of the Earth.* Hillside, NJ: Enslow, 1993.

Javna, John. *50 Simple Things Kids Can Do to Save the Earth.* Kansas City, MO: Andrews and McMeel, 1990.

Kerven, Rosalind. *Saving Planet Earth.* New York: Watts, 1992.

Kimball, Debi. *Recycling in America: A Reference Handbook.* Santa Barbara, CA: ABC-Clio, 1992.

Landau, Elaine. *Endangered Plants.* New York: Watts, 1992.

Langone, John. *Our Endangered Earth: What We Can Do to Save It.* Boston: Little, Brown, 1992.

Lund, Herbert F., ed. *The McGraw-Hill Recycling Handbook.* New York: McGraw-Hill, 1993.

Markle, Sandra. *The Kids' Earth Handbook.* New York: Atheneum, 1991.

Miles, Betty. *Save the Earth: An Action Handbook for Kids.* New York: Knopf, 1991.

Morgan, Nina. *The Plant Cycle.* New York: Thomson Learning, 1993.

Pope, Joyce. *Plant Partnerships.* New York: Facts on File, 1990.

———. *Practical Plants.* New York: Facts on File, 1990.

Pringle, Laurence P. *Living Treasure: Saving Earth's Threatened Biodiversity.* New York: Morrow, 1991.

———. *Saving Our Wildlife.* Hillside, NJ: Enslow, 1990.

Reader, John. *Man on Earth.* Austin: University of Texas Press, 1988.

Reading, Susan. *Desert Plants.* New York: Facts on File, 1990.

———. *Plants of the Tropics.* New York: Facts on File, 1990.

Rousmaniere, John, ed. *The Enduring Great Lakes.* New York: Norton, 1979.

Scott, Michael. *Ecology.* New York: Oxford University Press, 1995.

Seredich, John, ed. *Your Resource Guide to Environmental Organizations.* Irvine, CA: Smiling Dolphins Press, 1991.

Steloff, Rebecca. *Recycling.* New York: Chelsea House, 1991.

Suzuki, David T., and Barbara Hehner. *Looking at Plants.* New York: Wiley, 1992.

Taylor, Barbara. *Green Thumbs Up: The Science of Growing Plants.* New York: Random House, 1992.

Turiel, Isaac. *Indoor Air Quality and Human Health.* Stanford, CA: Stanford University Press, 1985.

Wallace, Arthur. *The Green Machine: Ecology and the Balance of Nature.* Oxford, England: Basil Blackwell, 1990.

The following books will help give you a broad understanding of volunteerism and opportunities in community service.

Berkowitz, Bill. *Local Heroes: The Rebirth of Heroism in America.* Lexington, MA: Lexington Books (D.C. Heath), 1987.

Buckley, William F., Jr. *Gratitude: Reflections on What We Owe to Our Country.* New York: Random House, 1990.

Coles, Robert. *The Call of Service: A Witness to Idealism.* Boston: Houghton Mifflin, 1993.

Daloz, Laurent A., Cheryl H. Keen, James P. Keen, and Sharon Daloz Parks. *Common Fire: Lives of Commitment in a Complex World.* Boston: Beacon Press, 1996.

Ellis, Susan J., and Katherine H. Noyes. *By the People: A History of Americans as Volunteers.* San Francisco: Jossey-Bass, 1990.

————. *The Volunteer Recruitment Book.* Philadelphia: Energize, Inc., 1994.

Grashow, Mark. *How to Make New York a Better Place to Live.* New York: City and Company, 1994.

Griggs, John, ed. *Simple Acts of Kindness: Volunteering in the Age of AIDS.* New York: United Hospital Fund of New York, 1989.

Lewis, Barbara. *The Kid's Guide to Service Projects.* Minneapolis: Free Spirit, 1993.

Luks, Allan, with Peggy Payne. *The Healing Power of Doing Good: The Health and Spiritual Benefits of Helping Others.* New York: Fawcett Columbine, 1991.

Olasky, Marvin. *Renewing American Compassion.* New York: The Free Press (Simon & Schuster), 1996.

Salzman, Marian, and Teresa Reisgies. *150 Ways Teens Can Make a Difference.* Princeton, NJ: Peterson's Guides, 1991.

Spaide, Deborah. *Teaching Your Kids to Care: How to Discover and Develop the Spirit of Charity in Your Children.* Secaucus, NJ: Carol Publishing Group, 1995.

Tarshis, Lauren. *Taking Off: Extraordinary Ways to Spend Your First Year Out of College.* New York: Fireside (Simon & Schuster), 1989.

Wuthnow, Robert. *Acts of Compassion: Caring for Others and Helping Ourselves.* Princeton, NJ: Princeton University Press, 1991.

APPENDIX A

The Nature Conservancy Regional and State Field Offices

Regional Offices

Eastern Region	(617) 542-1908
Midwest Region	(612) 331-0700
Southwest Region	(919) 967-5493
Western Region	(303) 444-1060
Latin America	(703) 841-5300
Pacific Region	(808) 537-4508

State Offices

Alabama	(205) 251-1155
Alaska	(907) 276-3133
Arizona	(520) 622-3861
Arkansas	(501) 663-6699
California	(415) 777-0487
Colorado	(303) 444-2950
Connecticut	(860) 344-0716
Delaware	(302) 369-4144
Florida	(407) 682-3664
Georgia	(404) 873-6946
Hawaii	(808) 537-4508
Idaho	(208) 726-3007
Illinois	(312) 346-8166
Indiana	(317) 923-7547
Iowa	(515) 244-5044
Kansas	(913) 233-4400
Kentucky	(606) 259-9655
Louisiana	(504) 338-1040
Maine	(207) 729-5181
Maryland	(301) 656-8673
Massachusetts	(617) 423-2545
Michigan	(517) 332-1741
Minnesota	(612) 331-0750
Mississippi	(601) 355-5357
Missouri	(314) 968-1105
Montana	(406) 443-0303

Nebraska	(402) 342-0282
Nevada	(702) 737-8744
New Hampshire	(603) 224-5853
New Jersey	(908) 879-7262
New Mexico	(505) 988-3867
New York	
New York Region	(518) 463-6133
New York City	(212) 997-1880
Adirondacks	(518) 576-2082
Central/ Western NY	(716) 546-8030
Eastern	(518) 272-0195
Long Island	(516) 367-3225
Lower Hudson	(914) 244-3271
South Fork/ Shelter Island	(516) 329-7689
North Carolina	(919) 403-8558
North Dakota	(701) 222-8464
Ohio	(614) 717-2770
Oklahoma	(918) 585-1117
Oregon	(503) 230-1221
Pennsylvania	(610) 834-1323
Rhode Island	(401) 331-7110
South Carolina	(803) 254-9049
South Dakota	(605) 331-0619
Tennessee	(615) 255-0303
Texas	(210) 224-8774
Utah	(801) 531-0999
Vermont	(802) 229-4425
Virginia	(804) 295-6106
Washington	(206) 343-4344
West Virginia	(304) 345-4350
Wisconsin	(608) 251-8140
Wyoming	(307) 332-2971